The Concise Theological Dictionary

BookCap™ Study Guides

www.bookcaps.com

© 2011. All Rights Reserved.

Table of Contents

A 4

B 14

C 17

D 24

E 30

F 35

G 38

H 40

I 44

J 48

K 49

L 50

M 52

N 57

O 59

P 62

Q	70
R	70
S	74
T	80
U	85
W	87
Z	88

A

A priori [ey-pry-awr-ee] -adj- Something which exists in the mind before it is experienced

A posteriori [ey-pos-teer-ee-awr-ee] -adj- Something which does not exist in the mind before it is experienced

Abba [ah-bah] -noun- A bishop who is Syriac or Coptic

Abaddon [uh-bad-n] -noun- A place full of destruction such as the depths of hell

Absolution [ab-suh-loo-shun] -noun- In Roman Catholic Theology, a priest's remission of sin or punishment because they were given the authority by God to make such a decision

Abyss [uh-bis] -noun- Referring to anything which is infinite or profound, such as the infernal regions of hell

Acosmism [uh-coz-miz-m] -noun- A view that God is the only reality and everything else ceases to exist independently

Active Obedience [ak-tic oh-bee-dee-ens -noun- The totality of Jesus Christ's actions, which Christians believe was in perfect obedience to the Law of God

Actual Grace [ak-chu-al gray-s] -noun- In Roman Catholic Theology, a share in God's life

Actual Sin [ak-chu-al sin] -noun- An individuals propensity to sin of his or her own free will

Adam [ad-uhm] -noun- In the bible, the first man God created

Adam, The Last [ad-uhm tha last] -noun- In the bible, the second Adam, or the second man created

Adiaphora [ey-dee-uh-for-uh] -noun- In Christianity, matters which are not essential to the faith but are still permissible

Adonai [uh-don-ay] -noun- A title of reverence for God, serving also as a substitute pronunciation of the Tetragrammaton

Adoptionism [uh-dop-shun-iz-uhm] -noun- The belief that Jesus Christ was the adopted, rather than natural, son of God

Advent [ad-vent] -noun- The birth of Christ into the world

Agnosticism [ag-nos-tuh-siz-uhm] -noun- A doctrine of uncertainty to any and all claims of superior knowledge

Albigenses [al-bi-jen-seez] -noun- Members of a Catharistic sect in the South of France that arose in the 11th century and was exterminated in the 13th century by a crusade and the inquisition

Amillennialism [ey-mill-en-ee-al-iz-uhm] -noun- The rejection of the theory that Christ will have a thousand-year long physical reign on the earth

Amyraldianism [ey-mer-al-dee-an-iz-m] -noun- A modified form of Calvinist theory which replaces the doctrine of limited atonement with a doctrine of unlimited atonement

Anabaptists [an-uh-bap-tizts] -noun- Protestant Christians of the Radical Reformation of 16th century Europe who reject many traditional Christian practices

Anamnesis [an-am-nee-sis] -noun- A prayer in a Eucharistic service which recalls the passion, resurrection, and ascension of Christ

Anathema [uh-nath-uh-muh] -noun- A person or thing which will be damned

Angelology [eyn-jel-ol-uh-jee] -noun- A doctrine or theory pertaining to angels

Anhypostasis [an-hip-oh-stay-sis] -noun- The idea that the logos' human nature did not subsist apart from the divine nature

Animism [an-uh-miz-uhm] -noun- The belief that personalized, supernatural beings often inhabit ordinary animals and objects, governing their existence

Annihilationism [uh-nahy-uh-ley-shuhn-iz-uhm] -noun- The Christian belief that when humans die they face total destruction rather than everlasting torment

Annunciation [uh-nun-see-ey-shuhn] -noun- The announcement that the Virgin Mary had conceived Christ, by Gabriel

Anthropic Principle [an-throh-pik prin-si-puhl] -noun- A cosmological theory that the life that is present on the universe dictated the way the universe evolved

Anthropocentrism [an-thruh-poh-sen-triz-uhm] -noun- A theory which regards human beings as the center of the universe

Anthropomorphic [an-thruh-puh-mawr-fik] -adj- Resembling human form or ascribing human qualities even if the thing is not human

Antedeluvian [an-tee-de-loo-vee-uhn] -noun- The period of time in the bible between the Creation and the Flood

Antichrist [an-ti-krahyst] -noun- A person who is often of power and who appears to be a major antagonist of Christ

Antinomianism [an-ti-noh-mee-uhn-iz-uhm] -noun- The idea that Christians are free from moral law by virtue of grace, as per the gospel

Apocalypse [uh-pok-uh-lips] -noun- A prophetic revelation which leads to the triumph of good over evil

Apocrypha [uh-pok-ruh-fuh] -noun- Religious writings which are seen by some to be inspired and inspiring but rejected by authorities

Apollyon [uh-pol-yuhn] -noun- The angel of the bottomless pit

Apologetics [uh-pol-uh-jet-iks] -noun- In theology, a branch concerned with defending the existence of Christ

Apologist [uh-pol-uh-jist] -noun- An author of the early Christian apologies which defended the faith

Apollinarianism [uh-pol-uh-nair-ee-uhn-iz-uhm] -noun- The view that while Jesus had a human body he could not have had a human mind, but a divine mind

Apostasy [uh-pos-tuh-see] -noun- A person's total desertion of their religious beliefs

Apostle [uh-pos-uhl] -noun- A person who was an early follower of Jesus and who helped to spread Christianity to the world

Apparition [ap-uh-rish-uhn] -noun- A supernatural appearance or something which is remarkable, such as a ghost

Archangel [ahrk-eyn-jehl] -noun- A chief angel; one of the nine celestial attendants of God

Argument from Design [ar-gyoo-ment fruhm dee-zayhn] -noun- An argument in the existence of God based on purpose in the universe and apparent design

Argumentum ad hominem [ar-gyoo-ment-uhm ad hom-uh-nuhm] -noun- An argument which shows that the statement of a person is not consistent with their supposed beliefs

Argumentum ad judicium [ar-gyoo-ment-uhm ad joo-dish-uhm] -noun- An argument which appeals to the judgment given

Argumentum ad populum [ar-gyoo-ment-uhm ad pop-yoo-luhm] -noun- An argument which is based on what most people think or belief to be true, but is usually false

Argumentum ad verecundiam [ar-gyoo-ment-uhm ad ver-uh-kuhn-dee-uhm] -noun- An argument of appeal to the authorities which is often false but can be persuasive

Ark [ahrk] -noun- A boat which was built by Noah and housed himself, his family, and a pair of every sort of animal to carry them through the flood

Ark of the Covenant [ahrl uhv tha kuhv-uh-nent] -noun- A box which contains the two tablets on which were written the ten commandments, which was carried by the Israelites through the desert to find Exodus

Arianism [ai -ee-uh-niz-uhm] -noun- The idea that Christ as the Son of God did not always exist, but that he was created by God the Father and therefore they are distinctly different

Armageddon [ahr-muh-ged-n] -noun- The final and completely destruction battle of the universe

Arminianism [ahr-min-ee-uh-niz-uhm] -noun- The doctrine stating that Christ died for all of the people rather than just the elect

Ascended Master [uh-sen-did mas-ter] -noun- People who in past lives were ordinary human being but who since have become enlightened through spiritual transformation

Ascension [uh-sen-shuhn] -noun- The body of Christ ascending from Heaven to Earth

Aspersion [uh-spur-zhuhn] -noun- The act of slandering or stating derogatory remarks or criticism

Assumption [uh-suhmp-shun] -noun- Taking something for granted or supposing something to be the truth

Assumption of Mary [uh-suhmp-shun uhv mer-ee] -noun- The taking of Mary's body up to Heaven after her death

Assurance [uh-shoor-uhns] -noun- Self-confidence, a positive declaration to promote confidence, or a promise or pledge

Astral Projection [as-truhl proh-jek-shun] -noun- A means of interpreting an out-of-body experience, by explanation of an astral body which is separate from the physical body and is capable of travelling outside of the physical body

Atheism [ey-thee-iz-uhm] -noun- A disbelief in any supreme beings, especially God

Atheism, Negative [ey-thee-iz-uhm neg-uh-tiv] -noun- The belief that there are not deities of any kind

Atheism, Positive [ey-thee-iz-uhm pohz-uh-tiv] -noun- The belief that there is no God

Aura [awr-uh] -noun- A pervasive quality which is thought to be emanating from a person or thing

Autonomy [aw-ton-uh-mee] -noun- The condition of being independent and of having free will

B

B.C. -noun- An abbreviation for "Before Christ", meaning the years before the birth of Christ

B.C.E. -noun- An abbreviation for "Before the Common Era" or "Before the Christian Era"

Baal [bey-uhl] -noun- A false god, or local Semitic deities which are worshipped sensually

Babel [bey-buhl] -noun- An ancient city in Shinar where a tower was built for the purpose of reaching Heaven

Babel, Tower of [tou-er uhv bey-buhl] -noun- A tower built in the city of Shinar which was meant to reach Heaven

Backsliding [bak-slahyd-ing] -verb- Relapsing into old habits which may be sinful or illegal

Baptism [bap-tiz-uhm] -noun- A ceremony which initiates a person into the church of Christianity by immersion in water or the application of water

Baptism, Believer's [bee-lee-vurs bap-tiz-uhm] -noun- A ceremony in which a person who has professed his or her faith in Jesus Christ is baptized, rather than the typical baptism which is performed on children at the request of their parents

Baptism for the Dead [bap-tiz-uhm fohr tha ded] -noun- When a living person is baptized on behalf of a person who has died so the living person will be free to act as the deceased's proxy

Baptismal Regeneration [bap-tiz-muhl ree-jen-uh-rey-shuhn] -noun- The idea of being baptized to achieve salvation; being "born again"

Beatitudes [beet-i-toods] -noun- A set of teachings by Jesus and expressed in the books of Matthew and Luke, referred to as the eight blessings

Beautification [byoo-tuh-fuh-key-shuhn] -noun- The act of making something beautiful

Beelzubub [beel-zuh-buhb] -noun- In Christianity and the bible he is one of the seven princes of Hell; a demon

Blasphemy [blas-fuh-mee] -noun- The act of a person believing they have the rights and privileges of God

Blessed Sacrament [bless-id sak-ruh-ment] -noun- A devotional name which refers to the Host after it has been consecrated in the Sacrament

Book of Life [buhk uhv lahyf] -noun- The book in which God has written the names of everyone who is destined to go to Heaven

Born Again [bohrn uh-gen] -noun- A spiritual rebirth of the human spirit; often those who have been born again feel as though they have a personal relationship with Jesus

Brazen Serpent [brey-zen sur-pent] -noun- A brass snake upon a pole which was made by Moses

Bride of Christ [brahyd uhv krahyst] -noun- Also known as the Lamb's wife, the Bride of Christ is introduced in the New Testament as Christ is often referred to as the "Bridegroom"

British Israelism [brit-ish iz-rey-uhl-iz-uhm] -noun- A believe that people of Great Britain are direct descendants of the Ten Lost Tribes of Israel

C

C.E. -noun- An abbreviation meaning "Common Era" or "Christian Era"

Caesar [see-zer] -noun- An emperor, dictator, or particularly powerful ruler such as Julius Caesar

Calvary [kal-vuh-ree] -noun- Also known as Golgotha or the place where Jesus faced his crucifixion

Calvinism [kal-vuh-niz-uhm] -noun- The doctrine of John Calvin which states that God is the supreme authority and so are the Scriptures

Canon [kan-uhn] -noun- The rules, principles, and standards of ecclesiastical law

Capital punishment [kap-uh-tahl pun-ish-ment] -noun- The punishment of the death penalty for a crime

Celestial Law [suh-les-chuhl] -noun- The full obedience of every law that comes from the mouth of God

Cessationism [ses-ey-shuhn-iz-uhm] -noun- The idea that the gifts of the Holy Spirit stopped being shared or practiced early on in the history of the Church

Chakra [chuhk-ruh] -noun- In yoga, one of the seven centers of spiritual energy within the body

Charismatic Gifts [kair-iz-mat-ik gifts] -noun- Spiritual gifts which are given by the Holy Spirit and which Christians need in order to fulfill the church's mission

Cherub/Cherubim [chair-uhb] -noun- Spiritual beings who are in the second order of angels

Chiliasm [kil-ee-az-uhm] -noun- Millennialism; A doctrine stating that Christ is going to return to earth to reign for 1000 years

Christian [kris-chuhn] -adj- Pertaining to or believing in Jesus Christ and his teachings

Christology [kri-stol-uh-jee] -noun- In theology, a branch which is concerned with nature and the deeds of Christ

Circumcision [sur-kuhm-sizh-uhn] -noun- The surgical removal of the foreskin in males as a religious rite

Cities of refuge [si-tees uhv ref-yooj] -noun- Towns inside of the Kingdom of Israel and the Kingdom of Judah where those who were accused of manslaughter could claim asylum

Clergy [klur-jee] -noun- In religion, a group of people who are ordained

Codex [koh-deks] -noun- A manuscript of the ancient Scriptures

Commercial Theory [kuh-mer-shuhl thee-ree] -noun- The theory that sin robbed God of his honor and therefore God's honor was restored through atonement of sinners

Common Grace [kom-uhn grays] -noun- A reference to the grace of God as common to all humankind or common to all people within a certain sphere of influence

Communicatio idiomatum [kom-yoo-nuh-kah-shee-oh id-ee-oh-mah-tuhm] -noun- A term which is aimed at explaining the way deity and humanity interact in the incarnation of Jesus

Communicatio Essentiae [kom-yoo-nuh-kah-shee-oh-es-sen-shee-uh] -noun- A belief that the communication of the essence of God is transferred in the Holy Trinity

Communion [kuh-myoon-yuhn] -noun- The elements of the Eucharist and the act of receiving them

Complimentarianism [kom-pluh-men-ter-ee-uhn-iz-uhm] -noun- The idea that while men and women have different roles in family, religion, and marriage, these roles are complimentary to one another

Concomitance [kon-kom-i-tuhns] -noun- In the Eucharist bread, the combination of the body and blood of Christ

Concupiscence [kon-kyoo-puh-suhns] -noun- Sexual desire, longing, or lust

Condemnation [kon-dem-ney-shuhn] -noun- The act of expressing an adverse judgment on something

Condign Merit [kon-dayhn mer-it] -noun- In Roman Catholicism, the signifying of merit with the dignity and virtues of Christ

Conditional immortality [kon-dish-uhn-uhl im-mohr-tal-uh-tee] -noun- A concept which states that salvation is only an option under the condition that the person being saved believes in Jesus

Congruent Merit [kon-groo-uhnt mer-it] -noun- The goodness which is bestowed upon one person resulting from the actions of another

Congregation [kong-gri-gey-shuhn] -noun- An organization or group of people which is brought together for a common purpose, such as religion and worship

Consecrate [kon-si-kreyt] -verb- To declare something as sacred

Consequentialism [kon-suh-kwen-shuh-liz-uhm] -noun- The idea that human's derive their moral worth from the consequences of their actions

Consubstantiation [kon-suhb-stan-shee-ey-shuhn] -noun- The doctrine which states that the body and blood of Christ are present in the bread and wine of the Eucharist

Contingent [kuhn-tin-juhnt] -adj- Something which happens without a known cause

Contrition [kuhn-trish-uhn] -noun- A complete and sincere remorse for one's sins

Coptic [kop-tik] -noun- A language which descended from Ancient Egypt though now it only exists in the Coptic Church

Corban [kawr-buhn] -noun- Especially among the ancient Hebrews, an offering or sacrifice made to God

Cosmological argument [koz-muh-log-i-kuhl ahr-gyoo-ment] -noun- The argument that God exists because the existence of the universe requires that there be an external cause as well

Cosmology [koz-mol-uh-jee] -noun- In philosophy and astronomy, the branch which deals with the origin, evolution, and structure of the universe

Covenant [kuhv-uh-nuhnt] -noun- Between the members of the church, a solemn agreement to act together in harmony and with the gospel

Creationism [kree-ey-shuh-niz-uhm] -noun- The doctrine which states that all things were created by God rather than evolution

Crucifixion [kroo-suh-fik-shuhn] -noun- Jesus' death upon the cross

D

Damnation [dam-ney-shuhn] -noun- As a punishment to sin, being condemned to eternal punishment

Deacons [dee-kuhn] -noun- An elected officer of a church; in hierarchical churches, an official who is next to a priest in the clerical order

Dead Sea Scrolls [ded-see-skrohls] -noun- Scrolls of leather, papyrus, and copper scrolls which contain partial texts from some books of the Old Testament as well as some non-biblical scrolls

Decalogue [dek-uh-lawg] -noun- The Ten Commandments

Decrees, of God [dih-kree] -noun- An eternal purpose of God

Decretive Will [dek-ruh-tiv will] -noun- God's sovereign will by which God passes whatever he wants by his divine decree

Deism [dee-iz-uhm] -noun- Belief that there is a God who created the world but since creation has become indifferent

Deity [dee-i-tee] -noun- A god or goddess, or the rank of a god

Demigod [dem-ee-god] -noun- In mythology, a being which is part human and part god

Deontology [dee-on-tol-uh-jee] -noun- A branch of ethics which deals with moral obligations and duties

Deposit of Faith [dih-poz-it] -noun- Jesus Christ's revelation which is passed on between two forms, the Sacred Scripture and Sacred Tradition

Depravity [dih-prav-i-tee] -noun- The state of being morally corrupt

Determinism [dih-tur-muh-niz-uhm] -noun- A doctrine which states that all events in life serve a purpose and have meaning

Deutero Isaiah [doo-te-oh ey-zey-uh] -noun- A claim that parts of the book of Isaiah in the Old Testament were written later than others

Diaconate [dahy-ah-uh-nit] -noun- The office of a deacon

Diadem [dahy-uh-dem] -noun- A crown, or a royal authority or dignity

Diaspora [dee-as-per-uh] -noun- The scattering of the Jews into countries outside of Palestine, or the Jews who live in the countries outside of Palestine

Dichotomy [dahy-kot-uh-mee] -noun- A division of something into two parts, halves, kinds, or pairs

Didache [did-uh-kee] -noun- The Teaching of the Twelve Apostles; from the 1st-2nd century A.D. a treatise on Christian morality and practices

Didactics [dahy-dak-tik] -adj- Intended for instruction, especially to teach a moral lesson

Diocese [dahy-uh-seez] -noun- A bishop's district of jurisdiction

Disciple [dih-sahy-puhl] -noun- A follower of Christ, especially one of the twelve personal followers

Dispensation [dis-puhn-sey-shuhn] -noun- A divine appointment, favor, or arrangement, as though by God

Dittography [dih-tog-ruh-fee] -noun- In writing or printing, the reduplication of letters or syllables, usually by error

Divination [div-uh-ney-shuhn] -noun- The attempting to tell the future of events or to reveal knowledge which has been hidden, generally by means of the supernatural or the occult

Divinity [dih-vin-i-tee] -noun- The quality of having divine attributes, such as the deity or Godhood

Docetism [doh-see-tiz-uhm] -noun- In the Roman Catholic Church, a heresy which stated that Jesus was not fully human and that his sufferings were not entirely real

Documentary Hypothesis [dok-yoo-men-ter-ee hahy-poth-uh-sis] -noun- A theory that the Five Books of Moses were not written by one person but from separate narratives which were edited together

Dogma [dawg-muh] -noun- A specific doctrine or tenet which is laid down with authority, especially in the church

Donatism [don-uh-tiz-uhm] -noun- A sect which believed that the church must be full of saints rather than sinners and sacraments were invalid

Dormition [dohr-mish-uhn] -noun- Literally, falling asleep; Figuratively, death

Double Predestination [duh-buhl pree-de-stin-ey-shuhn] -noun- The idea that God has already predetermined those who will be damned and those who will be saved

Dowsing [dous-ing] -verb- A type of divination which is used to locate groundwater, gemstones, gravesites, as well as many other materials or objects

Dualism [doo-uh-liz-uhm] -noun- A belief that the human being is split into two different parts, being body and soul

Duli [doo-lee] -noun- A village development committee in Nepal

E

Ebionism [eb-ee-uh-niz-uhm] -noun- A sect of Jewish Christians during the first era of Christianity who saw Jesus as the messiah and followed Jewish laws and rites

Ecclesiology [ih-klee-zee-ol-uh-jee] -noun- The study of the church doctrine

Economic Trinity [ek-uh-nom-ik trin-i-tee] -noun- A doctrine which is concerned with how the Father, the Son, and the Holy Spirit relate to one another and relate to the world

Eden [eed-n] -noun- The place where Adam and Eve lived until the Fall occurred

Efficacy [ef-i-kuh-see] -noun- The capacity of something to achieve the desired effect or result

Egalitarianism [ih-gal-i-tair-ee-uhn-iz-uhm] -noun- The belief that all people are equal, especially in the areas of political, social, and economic life

Eisegesis [ahy-si-jee-sis] -noun- An interpretation of Scripture which expresses the interpreter's own ideas rather than the actual meaning of the text

Elder [el-der] -noun- A layperson in the Protestant church who is acts as a governing officer and sometimes assists the pastor in matters

Elohim [e-loh-him] -noun- God, especially in terms of the Hebrew text of the Old Testament

Embryonic Recapitulation [em-bree-yon-ik-ree-kuh-pit-choo-ley-shuhn] -noun- The theory that each human's embryonic development represents the stages of evolution and evolutionary development

Empiricism [em-pir-uh-siz-uhm] -noun- A doctrine which states that all knowledge comes from sense experience

Entropy [en-truh-pee] -noun- A doctrine pertaining to overall social decline degeneration which is inevitable

Epistemology [ih-pis-tuh-mol-uh-jee] -noun- In philosophy, the branch which investigates human knowledge and its origins, methods, nature, and limits

Epistle [ih-pis-uhl] -noun- In the New Testament, one of the apostolic letters; or a reading as part of a Eucharistic service

Equivocation [ih-kwiv-uh-key-shuhn] -noun- To use of an ambiguous expression for the purpose of misleading

Erastianism [ih-ras-chuh-niz-uhm] -noun- A doctrine named from Thomas Erastus which stated the supremacy of the state over the church when it comes to ecclesiastical matters

Eschatology [es-kuh-tol-uh-jee] -noun- Doctrines which concern a person's final matters, such as death, judgment, and future state

Eschaton [es-kut-ton] -noun- The end of all time; the end of the world

Essenes [es-eens] -noun- A person who is a member of a Palestinian sect which believes in asceticism and celibacy

Essentia [es-sen-chee-uh] -noun- The substance of character which makes God what he is

Eternal Generation [ee-ter-nuhl jen-uh-rey-shuhn] -noun- One of the doctrines which forms the basis of the Holy Trinity and is present in reformation

Eucharist [yoo-kuh-rist] -noun- In Holy Communion, the consecrated elements, especially the bread

Eunuch [yoo-nuhk] -noun- A man who has been castrated, especially a man who was once appointed as a harem guard or palace official by an Oriental ruler

Eutychianism [yoo-tee-chee-uhn-iz-uhm] -noun- A doctrine belonging to Eutyches as well as his followers

Evolution, Theistic [thee-iz-tik ev-uh-loo-shuhn] -noun- A concept which states that the classical teachings of God are in line with the evolutionary view of modern science

Ex-Nihilo [eks-nahy-i-lo] -noun- In Latin, "out of nothing" which alludes to the idea that the earth was created out of nothing

Ex opere operato [eks-oh-per-oh-per-ah-toh] -noun- In Latin, "from the work done" which means that the efficacy of the Sacrament does not come from the holiness of the priest but rather of Christ himself

Example Theory [ek-zam-puhl-thee-ree] -noun- The idea that Jesus did not need to die for the sins of others, but rather others should see his sacrifice as a reason to repent and live life Christ-like

Excommunication [eks-kuh-myoo-nuh-key-shuhn] -noun- Literally, putting somebody out of communion; used as censure to deprive a person of membership within their community

Exegesis [ek-si-jee-sis] -noun- A critical analysis or interpretation of a text, especially of the Bible

Existentialism [eg-zi-sten-shuh-liz-uhm] -noun- A philosophy which stresses that a person is responsible for his or her own actions and must act as a self-determining agent

Exomologesis [eks-uh-mol-uh-jee-sis] -noun- A complete confession which usually occurs in public

Expiation [ek-spee-ey-shuhn] -noun- The means by which a person achieves reparation or atonement

Extreme Unction [ek-streem unk-shuhn] -noun- Also, the anointing of the sick; a sacrament, using oil and prayer, administered by a priest to someone who is sick or dying

F

Faith, Deposit of [duh-pos-it uhv fayth] -noun- The Apostle Constitution, by which Pope John Paul II ordered that the Catechism of the Catholic Church be published

False Prophets [fals-proh-fits] -noun- A person who falsely claims to be a prophet or who uses their prophetic gift for evil

Fatalism [feyt-l-iz-uhm] -noun- The idea that everything that happens is a result of fate and all things are inevitable

Fideism [fee-dey-iz-uhm] -noun- Reliance of all matters on faith, with the rejection of science of philosophy

Field of Blood [feeld uhv bluhd] -noun- Also Akeldama; a place in Jerusalem which has been associated with one of Jesus' followers, Judas Iscariot and where the land is made of reddish-colored clay, hence the name

Filioque [fil-ee-ok] -noun- In Latin, "and from the son"; a creed which states that the Holy Spirit proceeds from the Son and the Father

First-fruits [fur-st froots] -noun- The very first fruits ever produced which were offered to God, Adam, and the animals

Fission [fish-uhn] -noun- The act of splitting something into parts or cleaving

Foreordination [fawr-awr-dn-ey-shuhn] -noun- The predestination of some people to be given salvation, according to God

Foundationalism [fown-dey-shuhn-iz-uhm] -noun- Any theory which holds that beliefs are justified by what are known as basic beliefs

Four Spiritual Laws [fohr speer-i-choo-uhl laws] -noun- A booklet written in 1952 by Bill Bright which explains the essential laws of Christianity concerning salvation

Free Knowledge [free nol-ij] -noun- Knowledge which can be acquired, interpreted and applied freely

Freethinker [free thing-ker] -noun- A person who forms their opinions based on reason, rather than authority or tradition, especially a person who has different religious beliefs from the norm

Fusion [fyoo-zhuhn] -noun- The act of fusing things together; a coalition made up of many factions or parties

G

Gaia [gahy-uh] -noun- The goddess of the earth

Gammatria [gam-mat-ree-uh] -noun- In biblical numerology, the numerical value which is given to letters or strings of letters

Gap Theory [gap thee-ree] -noun- A form of Old Earth Creationism which notes that there may have been a gap of time between two creations in the first and the second verses of Genesis

Gehenna [gi-hen-uh] -noun- A place of extreme suffering and torment, such as the Valley of Hinnom where sacrifices were made to Moloch

General Revelation [jen-er-uhl rev-uh-ley-shuhn] -noun- A reference to the universality of God, including his knowledge and spirituality, which has been discovered through natural means

Gentile [jen-tahyl] -noun- A person who is not Jewish, especially a Christian; or a person amongst Mormons who is not Mormon

Gihon [zhee-hahn] -noun- A stream, and one of only four rivers of Eden

Gnosticism [nos-tuh-siz-uhm] -noun- A group of ancient heresies who believed that the realization of intuitive knowledge is the way to salvation of the soul

Godhead [god-hed] -noun- The holy trinity of God the Father, the Son, and the Holy Spirit

Gods, False [fals gods] -noun- A deity that is non-functioning or illegitimate despite its professed capabilities

Golgotha [gul-guh-thuh] -noun- The place where Jesus was crucified, on a hill near Jerusalem

Grace, Actual [ak-choo-uhl grays] -noun- Taking a share in God's like and having grace through actions

Grace, Sanctifying [sangk-tuh-fahy-ing grays] - noun- Grace which infuses with the soul at baptism and stays with the person through life to transform a once-sinner to a Holy Child of God

Great White Brotherhood [grayt wahyt bruhth-er-hood] -noun- According to New Age and Theosophical beliefs, a group of supernatural beings who have a great deal of power and who spread their teachings through certain selected humans

H

Hades [hey-deez] -noun- Hell; the underworld inhabited by the souls of the dead

Hadith [hah-deeth] -noun- In Islam, an account of things which were done or said by Muhammad as well as his companions or followers

Hamartiology [huh-mah-tee-ol-uh-jee] -noun- In Christianity, the doctrine of sin

Haplography [hap-log-ruh-fee] -noun- Accidentally leaving out a letter or group of letters which are supposed to repeated in a word

Hedonism [heed-n-iz-uhm] -noun- A doctrine which states that achieving pleasure is the highest good in life

Henotheism [hen-uh-thee-iz-uhm] -noun- The worshipping of one god while still believing in the existence of other gods

Heresy [her-uh-see] -noun- In the Roman Catholic Church, the rejection of an article of the church by one who has been baptized

Hermeneutics [her-muh-noo-tiks] -noun- The science and act of interpreting the Scriptures

Heterodoxy [het-er-uh-dok-see] -noun- Beliefs that are different from those which are Orthodox but do not qualify as heresy

Higher Self [hahy-er self] -noun- Also known as the "real you", higher self is achieved when each of the self's incarnations have gone on and achieved their main objectives

Hierology [hahy-uh-rol-uh-jee] -noun- A branch of learning or literature which pertains to sacred things

Holy Orders [hoh-lee ohr-ders] -noun- The ordination of individuals to fit certain special roles within the ministry

Holy Spirit [hoh-lee speer-it] -noun- The spirit or presence of God in regards to the religious experience of an individual

Homiletics [hom-uh-let-iks] -noun- The art of preaching or of writing and giving sermons

Homoiousios -noun- The idea that the Father and Son in both attributes and substance and that anyone who feels differently is guilty of heresy

Homoousios -noun- The idea that the Holy Trinity of the Father, the Son, and the Holy Spirit are distinctly separate yet coexist and ultimately form one being

Homophony [huh-mof-uh-nee] -noun- In linguistics, the phenomenon of words that come from different origins having the same sound

Host [hohst] -noun- At the celebration of the Eucharist, the water or bread which is consecrated

Humanism [hyoo-muh-niz-uhm] -noun- The idea that humanity moves forward due to its own efforts, rather than the power of religion

Hyper Calvinism [hahy-per-kal-vin-iz-uhm] -noun- The act of Calvinist ministers denying free offer of the gospel as well as duty-faith

Hyperdulia [hahy-per-doo-lee-uh] -noun- The act of honoring a saint, especially through respectful gestures such as making the sign of the cross in front of saintly relics or kissing a saintly icon or statue

Hypostasis [hahy-pos-tuh-sis] -noun- In terms of Christ, the state in which his two natures, both human and divine, are united into one being

Hypostatic Union [hahy-puh-stat-ik yoon-yuhn] -noun- In theology, the way to describe the act of hypostasis

Iconoclasm [ahy-klon-uh-klaz-uhm] -noun- The destruction of religious icons deliberately and usually motivated by religious or political beliefs

I

Idealism [ahy-dee-uh-liz-uhm] -noun- In philosophy, the idea that the mind, body, and spirit are the most fundamental governing agents and forms of reality

Ignosticism [ig-nos-tuh-siz-uhm] -noun- In theology, the belief that all other theological ideas are too assuming of God as a concept

Immaculate Conception [ih-mak-yoo-let kon-sep-shuhn] -noun- The belief that the Virgin Mary was conceived free from Original Sin and thus was preserved by God from conception

Image of God [im-ij uhv god] -noun- In Abrahamic religions, the belief that human beings are created in God's image are therefore are inherently valuable aside from their function

Immutability [im-yoo-tuh-bil-i-tee] -noun- The ability to remain unchanged or to deflect change

Impeccability [im-pek-uh-bil-i-tee] -noun- The ability to remain flawless and incapable of sin

Impute, Imputation [im-pyoo-tey-shuhn] -noun- An accusation of a fault or a crime and in terms of religion, a sin

Immortality [im-awr-tal-i-tee] -noun- The condition or quality of having an unending life

Imprimatur [im-pri-mah-ter] -noun- An official license, often given by the Roman Catholic Church, which is required to publish certain books, pamphlets, etc.

In facto [in fak-toh] -noun- A thing which exists and is complete

In fieri [in-fee-ree] -noun- A thing which is beginning to exist but has not yet achieved its complete form

Incarnation [in-kar-ney-shuhn] -noun- The doctrine which states that the second member of the Trinity took human form as Jesus Christ and thus Christ is both God and man

Incarnational Theology [in-kar-ney-shuhn-al thee-ol-uh-jee] -noun- The affirmation that the second member of the Trinity took the human form of Jesus Christ

Indefectibility [in-di-fek-tuh-bil-i-tee] -noun- The act of being faultless, or not liable to failure

Indulgence [in-duhl-juhns] -noun- The remission of a punishment for sin after the sin has been forgiven

Inerrancy [in-er-uhn-see] -noun- The belief that there is no error within the bible, in both matters of faith and matters of science

Infidel [in-fi-del] -noun- A person who has no religious faith or accepts no religious beliefs, especially Christianity

Infinity [in-fin-i-tee] -noun- An infinite amount of space, time, quality, number, quantity, or extent

Infralapsarianism [in-fruh-lap-sair-ee-uhn-iz-uhm] -noun- A doctrine stating that God planned creation, He permitted the fall, he chose a certain number and allowed their redemption, and he chose the others who would be eternally punished

Initium Fidei [in-ish-ee-uhm-fi-dey] -noun- In Latin, the beginning of faith; The first act of faith which is made by a Christian

Inspiration [in-spuh-rey-shuhn] -noun- A doctrine which states that the Bible was written by God's influence which means it is without error in its original form

Intelligent Design [in-tel-uh-jent de-zahyn] - noun- The belief that evolution cannot fully be responsible for every form of life on the planet because some biological structures are too complex

Intermediate state [in-ter-mee-dee-et dee-zahyn] -noun- The period of time between a person's death and resurrection, though the belief of what condition the person is in during that period of time is undetermined

Irresistible Grace [ir-i-zis-tuh-buhl] -adj- Not capable of being withstood, such as an urge, feeling, or action

J

Jehovah [ji-hoh-vuh] -noun- In the Old Testament, the name of God in reference to the Hebrew Scriptures

Jehovah's Witnesses [ji-hoh-vuhs wit-nis] -noun- A pseudo-Christian religion which rejects the traditional Christian doctrines as well as war and other religions

Jesuit [jezh-oo-it] -noun- A member of the Roman Catholic religious order which was founded in 1534 by Ignatius of Loyola

Jesus Seminar [jee-zus sem-uh-nahr] -noun- A group of about 150 people who meet and vote with colored beads on which of Jesus' supposed sayings are authentic, and also discuss the historical aspects of Jesus

Judgment [juhj-muhnt] -noun- The final trial which all people must go through, whether living or deceased, when the world comes to an end

K

Karma [kahr-muh] -noun- In Hinduism, the compilation of all actions in a person's life as well as in their past lives which results in that person being reincarnated at a level fit for all of their actions

Kathenotheism [kuh-then-uh-thee-iz-uhm] -noun- A person's worship of only one god at a time, despite the fact that they may believe in several gods

Kenosis [ki-noh-sis] -noun- A doctrine which states that Christ gave up his divine attributes for the sake of being able to experience human suffering

L

Laity [ley-i-tee] -noun- The laypeople of the church; members of the church who are not clergy

Latria [luh-trahy-uh] -noun- The most supreme form of worship, which may only be available for God to practice

Law of Excluded Middle [law uhv eks-cloo-did mid-duhl] -noun- One of the three basic laws of logic which states that every statement is either true or false, there is no middle

Law of Identity [law uhv ay-den-ti-tee] -noun- A law stating that each proposition suggests and implies itself

Law of Non-Contradiction [law uhv non-kon-truh-di-shuhn] -noun- One of the basic laws of logic which states that it is not possible for a thing to be both true and not true when it is seen in the same context

Law of Proper Inference [law uhv prop-er in-fuhr-ents] -noun- One of the basic laws of logic which states that "A" must be equal to "C" if "A" is equal to "B" and "B" is equal to "C"

Laying on of hands [ley-ing-on-uhv-handz] -noun- According to the New Testament, when an elder is ordinated hands are laid on him to transfer power and authority

Lent [lent] -noun- Beginning at Ash Wednesday and lasting until Easter, the period of forty days which is usually accompanied by a fast of some sort or prayer

Liberalism [lib-er-uh-liz-uhm] -noun- In Protestantism, a movement which advocates freedom from authority and tradition in order to accept some scientific views and conceptions

Limited atonement [lim-i-ted uh-tohn-ment] - noun- In the teachings of Reformed Christianity, the belief that Jesus did not atone for the sins of all, but rather only the sins of the elect

Liturgy [lit-er-jee] -noun- A ritual of public worship, such as the Eucharist, especially in the Eastern Church

Logic [loj-ik] -noun- A study of the principles of reasoning in any branch of knowledge

Logos [loh-gos] -noun- Sometimes refers to the second of the Trinity, the Son; literally meaning "the word"

M

Mammon [mam-uhn] -noun- Either material wealth and riches, or the personification of riches in the form of a deity

Mantra [man-truh] -noun- In Hinduism, a word or formula which is chanted as a prayer or incantation

Materialism [muh-teer-ee-uh-liz-uhm] -noun- The belief that the only things that truly exist are those which are material

Martyr [mahr-ter] -noun- A person who would gladly suffer and die rather than renounce his or her religion

Mass [mas] -noun- Performed by a priest, mass is the reenactment of the sacrifice of Christ which involves the consecration of bread and wine into the body and blood of Christ

Means of Grace [meens uhv grays] -noun- Generally considered to be the Lord's Supper, the Gospel, and baptism; a manner which grace is imparted to the taker of the sacrifice

Mediation, Mediator [mee-dee-ey-shuhn] -noun- A person who intervenes and conciliates, such as Moses or Jesus

Megiddo [muh-gid-oh] -noun- In North Israel, an ancient city which is often associated with the Biblical Armageddon

Merit [mer-it] -noun- A person's worthiness of receiving a spiritual reward which will be acquired under the influence of grace

Messiah [mi-sahy-uh] -noun- The person who is both promised and expected to deliver the Jewish people; Jesus Christ

Metaphysics [met-uh-fiz-iks] -noun- In philosophy, the branch which deals with the first principles of knowing and of being

Middle Knowledge [mid-duhl nol-ij] -noun- The knowledge that God knows what actions individuals will take and that he will deal with them in each set of circumstances

Millennium [mi-len-ee-uhm] -noun- A period of one thousand years; it is said that there will be one thousand years when Christ will reign on the earth

Minor Prophets [mahy-ner prof-its] -noun- In the Old Testament, the Minor Prophets are the twelve shortest stories.

Minuscule [min-uh-skyool] -noun- A type of Greek writing where the letters are all lower case

Modalism [moh-duh-liz-uhm] -noun- A theological error which states that there is one person only in the godhead and that one person manifests in three forms: the Father, the Son, and the Holy Spirit

Molinism [moh-luh-niz-uhm] -noun- In the idea of Middle Knowledge, Molinism expresses a belief that God knows what people will choose when exercising their free will and he chooses who will be saved based on this information

Monarchianism [muh-nahr-kee-uh-niz-uhm] -noun- A doctrine which maintains that God is one unified being made up of the Father, the Son, and the Holy Spirit

Monergism [mon-er-jiz-uhm] -noun- A doctrine stating that of the Holy Trinity, the Holy Spirit acts independently in terms of how human will effects regeneration

Monism [mon-iz-uhm] -noun- The theory that there is one single governing principle or causal factor in the universe which determines all actions and behaviors

Monolatry [muh-nol-uh-tree] -noun- An individual's worshipping of only one god despite acknowledging that more than one may exist

Monophysitism [muh-nof-uh-sahyt-iz-uhm] -noun- A doctrine which states that Christ has one nature though it is both human and divine

Monotheism [mon-uh-thee-iz-uhm] -noun- A doctrine stating that there is only one god in existence

Moral Influence Theory [mohr-uhl in-floo-ents thee-ree] -noun- A theory which states that Christ did not need to die to remove sin, but that the influence of his love should move sinners to repent

Mormonism [mawr-muhn-iz-uhm] -noun- The religious practice of those who belong to the Church of Latter Day Saints; a belief that denies the Trinity and believes that people have the potential to become gods or goddesses

Mortal Sin [mawr-tuhl sin] -noun- A serious transgression against god which is committed knowingly and willfully and which deprives any possibility of achieving grace

N

Natural Knowledge [nach-er-uhl nol-ij] -noun- The knowledge of God of all things in existence or in potential existence

Natural Theology [nach-er-uhl thee-ol-uh-jee] -noun- A means of studying God by the use of reason and observation of nature, and can often involve using logic to try to prove God's existence

Naturalism [nach-er-uhl-iz-uhm] -noun- A doctrine stating that a person can be saved by natural religion, or that religious truth comes from the study of natural processes

Naturalistic evolution [nach-er-uhl-iz-tik ev-uh-loo-shuhn] -noun- A theory that over billions of years everything on earth evolved naturally, without any divine intervention

Negative Atheism [neg-uh-tiv ey-thee-iz-uhm] -noun- A position of atheism which denies the existence of any gods; also known as weak atheism

Neo-orthodoxy [nee-oh-awr-thuh-dok-see] -noun- In Protestant theology, a movement which stresses the absolute sovereignty of God

New Atheism [noo ey-thee-iz-uhm] -noun- A form of atheism where not only is there a disbelief of God but also an aggressive attack of religion and a focus on science and reason in terms of determining ethics as well as truth

Nestorianism [ne-stawr-ee-uh-niz-uhm] -noun- A view that the human and divine natures of Jesus were not in contact with one another and thus it would be impossible to worship a human version of Jesus Christ

Nihil Obstat [nahy-hil ob-stat] -noun- In Roman Catholicism, the permission to publish a book after it has been officially determined to carry no information that goes against the teachings of religious faith or morals

Nihilism [nahy-uh-liz-uhm] -noun- In philosophy, the view that human life serves no purpose and has no meaning; the foundation of anarchy

Nile, The [tha nahyl] -noun- Referenced several times in the Bible, a river in Egypt which empties out into the Mediterranean Sea

Nun [nuhn] -noun- A woman who has pledged celibacy, poverty, and obedience to the Lord in the name of religion

O

Occam's Razor [ok-uhms rey-zer] -noun- In philosophy, a rule that everything should be explained in the simplest way possible

Occult [uh-kuhlt] -adj- Characteristic of the supernatural, astrology, magic, or beyond the ordinary range of understanding

Omnipotence [om-nip-uh-tuhns] -noun- The quality of having all of the power in the world, as God

Omnipresence [om-nuh-pres-uhns] -noun- Being capable of being in all places at all times, as God

Omniscience [om-nis-ee-uhns] -noun- Having all of the knowledge that is available in the world, as God

Ontological Argument [on-tl-oj-i-kuhl ahr-gyoo-ment] -noun- An argument to prove the existence of God, stating that because one can conceive that nothing greater than God can possibly exist then God must exist

Ontological Trinity [on-tl-oj-i-kuhl trin-i-tee] -noun- The teaching that all parts of the Holy Trinity are equal to one another

Ontology [on-tol-uh-jee] -noun- In philosophy and metaphysics, the branch which deals with the nature of being

Open Theism [oh-pen thee-iz-uhm] -noun- The idea that God has granted free will to all of humanity but in order for the will to truly be free God must not reveal the choices which will come in the future of a person's life

Oracles [awr-uh-kuhls] -noun- People who are capable of divine communication and who deliver wise and authoritative pronouncements

Ordain [awr-deyn] -verb- To decree something to happen, or to not happen; the power of God

Ordination [awr-dn-ey-shuhn] -noun- A ceremony which takes place one someone is ordained, that is, consecrated into the ministry

Ordo salutis [awr-do sal-oo-tis] -noun- In Latin, "order of salvation"; the order of the decrees God gives to grant salvation

Original Sin [awr-ij-uh-nuhl sin] -noun- The inheritance of sin from Adam which is passed down through the generations and the effect of this inheritance

Orthodoxy [awr-thuh-dok-see] -noun- An agreement with the Bible teachings and the standards of the doctrines within the Bible

Other, Wholly [ho-lee uh-ther] -noun- The difference between God and everything and everyone else

P

Paedocommunion [ped-oh-kuh-myoon-yuhn] -noun- A teaching that infants should be allowed communion because they are a part of the Old and New Testaments

Panentheism [pan-en-thee-iz-uhm] -noun- The belief that while God is comprised of many more things, the universe is contained within him

Pantheism [pan-thee-iz-uhm] -noun- In theology, a doctrine or belief that God is the reality of the universe while people are only manifestations

Papyrus [puh-pahy-ruhs] -noun- A writing material formed by taking the leaves of the Papyri plant and pressing them together; in Biblical times the Papyri plant grew on the banks of the Nile River

Parable [par-uh-buhl] -noun- A short story of allegory which serves the purpose of teaching a religious truth or moral lesson

Paradigm [par-uh-dahym] -noun- A set of assumptions or a framework of one's beliefs which are used to understand the world and the people on it

Parapsychology [par-uh-sahy-kol-uh-jee] -noun- In psychology, the branch which explores psychic phenomena and the supernatural

Parousia [puh-roo-zee-uh] -noun- Also, advent; the entrance of Christ into the world

Pascals Wager [pas-kals wey-jer] -noun- The idea that believing in God makes sense because if there is in fact a God and he is ignored the person doing the ignoring will be in trouble, and if God does not exist then it does not matter that he was falsely worshipped

Passive Obedience [pas-iv oh-bee-dee-uhns] -noun- A person's obedience to an authority without question, or a person's surrender of their will to another

Passover [pas-oh-ver] -noun- A festival which celebrates the freedom of the Jews from Egypt

Patriology [pah-tree-ol-uh-jee] -noun- The study of God the Father in the Holy Trinity

Patrology [puh-trol-uh-jee] -noun- In theology, a branch which deals with the teachings of the fathers of church and their early writings

Pedobaptism [ped-oh-bap-tiz-uhm] -noun- The baptism of an infant which by some views saves the infant

Pelagianism [puh-ley-jee-uh-niz-uhm] -noun- The teachings of Pelagius which deny the concept of original sin and believe that people have free will

Penance [pen-uhns] -noun- In Roman Cathoicism, a sacrament consisting of confession of sin with remorse and sorrow and expressed desire to make amends, followed by forgiveness

Penal Substitution [pee-nuhl suhb-sti-too-shuhn] -noun- A view which maintains that Jesus legally took on the punishment for all of the sinners

Pentateuch [pen-tuh-took] -noun- In the Old Testament, the first five books: Exodus, Genesis, Leviticus, Numbers, and Deuteronomy

Pentecost [pen-ti-kawst] -noun- The commemoration of the descending of the Holy Ghost upon the apostles, celebrating on the seventh Sunday after Easter

Permissive Decree pur-mis-iv de-kree] -noun- A decree which is given by God though is not direct; it is a decree which he gives permission to happen rather than by direct action of his will

Permissive Will   [pur-mis-iv will] -noun- A will which is not decreed by God to occur and is not in accordance with his law, but rather is the will of sin to occur

Perseverance [pur-suh-veer-uhns] -noun- A person's continuance of a state of grace until the end of their life, which leads to eternal salvation

Philosophy [fi-los-uh-fee] -noun- The critical study of the core principles of a certain branch of knowledge, especially with the intention of improving them

Pishon   [pish-uhn] -noun- One of the four rivers near Eden

Pluralism [ploor-uh-liz-uhm] -noun- A person's holding of more than one office at a time

Pneumatology [noo-muh-tol-uh-jee] -noun- A belief in supernatural spirits which act as intermediaries between humans and God

Polygamy [puh-lig-uh-mee] -noun- The practice of having more than one spouse at a time, usually pertaining to wives

Polytheism [pol-ee-thee-iz-uhm] -noun- The believe in more than one god

Positive Atheism [poz-uh-tiv ey-thee-iz-uhm] -noun- A claim made by some atheists that they know for sure that God does not exist

Postmillennialism [pohst-mil-en-ee-uh-liz-uhm] -noun- The belief that the entire world will convert to Christianity through the teaching of the word of God and that Jesus will return to Earth when this happens

Postmodernism [pohst-mod-ern-iz-uhm] -noun- A theory in which practices once thought as taboo are equal to traditional values in terms of validity

Pragmatism [prag-muh-tiz-uhm] -noun- In philosophy, whatever works is the best solution

Pre-Adamites [pree-ad-uhm-ahyts] -noun- A view that there were people on the world before Adam and Eve were created but they were destroyed when Satan fell

Preceptive Will [pree-sep-tiv-will] -noun- The will that God has for man, such as man does not lie, steal, or sin

Pre-existence [pree-eks-is-tuhns] -noun- The idea that there we existed before our time on earth, though not biblically

Predestine, Predestination [pree-des-tin-ey-shuhn] -noun- A doctrine stating that while God has predestined everything to happen he does not control sin

Premillennialism [pree-mil-en-ee-uh-liz-uhm] -noun- A teaching that Jesus will rule the world again for one thousand years where peace will reign and at the end of this time Satan will create an army to fight against Jesus

Presuppositionalism [pree-sup-uh-zish-uhn-al-iz-uhm] -noun- A branch of apologetics which asserts that the only basis for rational thought is Christianity

Preterism [pre-ter-iz-uhm] -noun- The view that nearly all things prophesized by Jesus in the Old Testament were made true by the destruction of the Jerusalem Temple in 70 A.D.

Preterition [pre-ter-ish-uhn] -noun- The act of passing something over, as God did to the people who were not predestined for salvation

Prevenient Grace [pree-ven-ee-ent grays] -noun- The grace that a person achieves before they decide to have belief in Jesus

Priest [preest] -noun- An ordained member of the pastoral office or clergy, such as a minister

Process Theology [proh-ses thee-ol-uh-jee] -noun- In theology, the position that God is always changing as is the people's knowledge of Him

Propitiation [pruh-pish-ee-ey-shuhn] -noun- The turning away of wrath by a certain offering, such as the blood of Jesus on the cross

Prostration [proh-strey-shuhn] -noun- The act of lower one's body in front of another person or an object, as if often done in church

Protoevangelium [proh-toh-ev-an-jel-ee-uhm] -noun- A prophecy which states that Christ will redeem mankind by overcoming the devil

Protestant [prot-uh-stuhnt] -noun- A follower of one of the Christian bodies which separated from Rome during the reformation

Purgatory [pur-guh-toh-ree] -noun- In Roman Catholicism, the place where a person spends their afterlife and becomes purged of some of their sins

Q

Qumran [koom-rahn] -noun- The place where the Dead Sea Scrolls were found, northeast of the Dead Sea

Quran, The [koo-rahn] -noun- Also the Koran; the sacred text of Islam

R

Rabbi, Rabonni [rab-ahy] -noun- In Judaism, the chief religious officer at a synagogue who is qualified to rule on any questions pertaining to Jewish law

Ransom Theory [ran-sum thee-ree] -noun- A theory or teaching that Jesus' death on the cross was payment, or ransom, to Satan

Rapture [rap-chur] -noun- An event which occurs when Christ returns and those who have followed him with truth and are still alive will be taken to meet God

Rationalism [rash-uh-nl-iz-uhm] -noun- The theory that human reason, with no divine intervention, is the only guide to religious truth

Recapitulation Theory [ree-kuh-pich-yoo-ley-shuhn thee-ree] -noun- A theory that Jesus went through all of the same experiences that Adam did, including his sins

Reconcile, Reconciliation [rek-uhn-sil-ee-ey-shuhn] -noun- The change in the relationship between God and man upon the death of Jesus

Redaction Criticism [ree-dak-shuhn krit-uh-siz-uhm] -noun- A theory that early publishers of the Bible altered or embellished its stories to achieve a more miraculous and spiritual tone

Redemption [ri-demp-shuhn] -noun- Salvation or the deliverance from sin

Regeneration [ri-jen-uh-rey-shuhn] -noun- A religious revival or a rebirth, spiritually

Reincarnation [ree-in-kahr-ney-shuhn] -noun- A believe that after a person dies their soul finds a way to come back to earth in some form

Relativism [rel-uh-tiv-iz-uhm] -noun- A theory which states that the material by which people are judged is all relative and depends on the person and the environment which they are in

Relic [rel-ik] -noun- A personal memorial of a saint or a martyr, such as their body, a portion of it, or something they owned which is preserved and worshipped

Religious Naturalaism [ri-lij-uhs nach-er-uh-liz-uhm] -noun- A branch of religion and philosophy in which the followers get their religious beliefs from science and reason and believe that all religions should be respected

Repentance [ri-pen-tns] -noun- A person's feeling of sorrow or contrition for past wrongdoings and sins

Replacement Theology [ri-pleys-muhnt thee-ol-uh-jee] -noun- A teaching which states that Israel was replaced by the Christian church in terms of God's purpose

Resurrection [rez-uh-rek-shuhn] -noun- To be raised from the dead, or the reception of a new body when Christ returns

Revelation [rev-uh-ley-shuhn] -noun- Something which is disclosed, such as God's will to His followers

Revelation, General [jen-uh-ruhl rev-uh-ley-shuhn] -noun- The revelation which is known by all, of God and what is seen as right and wrong

Revelation, Special [spesh-uhl rev-uh-ley-shuhn] -noun- A revelation of God as well as morality which is displayed in the Bible

Righteousness [rahy-chuhs-nis] -noun- A quality of absolute moral purity which belongs to God only

Rite [rahyt] -noun- A ceremonial or religious procedure or practice, such as the Eucharist service

Ritual [rich-oo-uhl] -noun- A ceremony which aims to mimic a past event, initiate a person into a belief system, or offer a sacrifice

Rosary [roh-zuh-ree] -noun- A string of beads which is used in religious prayer

S

Sacerdotalism [sas-er-doht-l-iz-uhm] -noun- The methods, system, or spirit of the priesthood

Sacrament [sak-ruh-muhnt] -noun- Of the Eucharist, the consecrated elements, especially the bread

Sacred Tradition [sey-krid truh-dish-uhn] -noun- A tradition in the Eastern Orthodox or Roman Catholic churches which has been handed down through generations

Sadducee [saj-uh-see] -noun- In Judaism, a Palestinian sect which took a literal translation of the Bible and rejected oral law and tradition

Saint [seynt] -noun- A person who is recognized by the church for exceptional holiness, virtue, and benevolence

Salvation [sal-vey-shuhn] -noun- Redemption or deliverance from the penalty of sin

Sanctify, Sanctification [sangk-tuh-fi-key-shuhn] -noun- The act of setting something apart from others to make it holy, sacred, and to consecrate it

Sanctifying Grace [sangk-tuh-fahy-ing grays] -noun- Grace which infuses with the soul at baptism and stays with the person through life to transform a once-sinner to a Holy Child of God

Sanhedrin [san-hed-rin] -noun- The highest council of Jews who had authority from the 2nd century B.C.

Savior [seyv-yer] -noun- A person who saves or delivers, like God

Scapular [skap-yuh-ler] -adj- A monastic garment which is loose and sleeveless and hangs from the shoulders

Scholasticism [skuh-las-tuh-siz-uhm] -noun- A method of study which was used in the middle ages and which used reason and logic to support the doctrine of the church

Scientific Naturalism [sahy-uhn-tif-ik nach-uh-ruhl-iz-uhm] -noun- A view that all components of the universe are to be studied in only natural terms

Scribe [skrahyb] -noun- In Judaism, the member of a group of scholars who was responsible for transcribing, editing, and interpreting the Bible

Second Coming, The [sek-uhnd kuh-ming] - noun- The term which applies to the coming of Christ back into the world, ascending from the Heavens

Selah [see-luh] -noun- An expression which occurs in the Psalms which is thought to be a direction to the orator to add inflection to the voice or to raise or lower it

Septuagint, The   [sep-too-uh-jint] -noun- The oldest version of the Old Testament, in Greek

Sign of the Cross [sahyn uhv tha kros] -noun- The movement of the hand to make the sign of the cross upon one's chest

Skepticism [skep-tuh-siz-uhm] -noun- A doubt or nonbelief in regards to a religion, especially Christianity

Socinianism [soh-sin-ee-uhn-iz-uhm] -noun- A branch of religion which rejects many classical doctrines of Christianity, such as the Trinity, original sin, and the Divinity of Christ

Sola Fide [soh-la-fahyd] -noun- The teaching that if a person puts all of his trust into Jesus' sacrifice that he will be saved

Sola Gratia [soh-la-grah-shuh] -noun- The idea that God pardons people based only on the sacrifice of Christ, rather than their own merit

Sola Scriptura [soh-la-skrip-chur-uh] -noun- An idea that the Scriptures hold all of the information one needs to achieve salvation and live a proper life in the eyes of God

Soli Deo Gloria [soh-lee-dey-oh-gloh-ree-uh] -noun- A teaching of the reformation which states that the only glory given should be given to God alone

Solus Christus [soh-luhs-kris-tuhs] -noun- A teaching of the reformation which states that salvation comes from Jesus and is of no human control

Soteriology [suh-teer-ee-ol-uh-jee] -noun- The doctrine of salvation, through Jesus Christ

Soul Sleep [sohl-sleep] -noun- The theory that when a person dies his soul no longer exists, but when the judgment day comes he is brought back to life for the sole purpose of being judged

Sovereignty [sov-rin-tee] -noun- An extreme and unrestricted power, such as that of God

Special Revelation [spesh-uhl rev-uh-ley-shuhn] -noun- A revelation of God as well as morality which is displayed in the Bible

Strict Merit [strikt-mer-it] -noun- A person's achieved goodness which is a direct reflection of their work

Subjectivism [sub-jek-tiv-iz-uhm] -noun- In philosophy, the view that every bit of knowledge and truth is subjective, based on the individual's interpretation of what is learned

Supernatural [soo-per-nach-er-uhl] -adj- Of something which is beyond the realm of what is natural or explainable by nature or phenomena

Supralapsarianism [soo-pruh-lap-ser-ee-uhn-iz-uhm] -noun- The idea that God first decided who to save from the world and then created the notion of sin and decided it would be allowed to exist

Synagogue [sin-uh-gog] -noun- In Judaism, a house of worship or a place for religious teachings

Synergism [sin-er-jiz-uhm] -noun- A doctrine which states that the Holy Ghost and human will work together for the sake of regeneration

Synoptic Gospels [sin-op-tik-gos-puhls] -noun- Matthew, Mark, and Luke; the first three gospels in the Bible

T

Tabernacle [tab-er-nak-uhl] -noun- A structure which God ordered be built for him so he would be able to live amongst his people if he so chose

Teleological argument [tel-ee-uh-loj-i-kuhl-awr-gyoo-muhnt] -noun- The theory that God must exist because the universe has a design and therefore must have a designer, which is God

Teleology [tel-ee-ol-uh-jee] -noun- A study of the evidence that there is a purpose to the design of nature

Terminism [ter-muh-niz-uhm] -noun- The idea that God may get to the point where he no longer desires the salvation of a person and from that moment that person can no longer be saved

Testament [test-uh-muhnt] -noun- A covenant between God and humans; either of the two sections of the Bible

Tetragrammaton [te-truh-gram-uh-ton] -noun- In Hebrew, the word meaning God

Theism [thee-iz-uhm] -noun- The believe in the existence of one or more gods

Theistic Evolution [thee-iz-tik-ev-uh-loo-shuhn] -noun- The idea that God used natural processes of evolution when he created the world as it is today

Theodicy [thee-od-uh-see] -noun- The study of evil and how something as holy as God could allow evil to exist

Theology [thee-ol-uh-jee] -noun- The study of divinity, divine things, religious truths, God, and God's connection to the universe

Theonomy [thee-on-uh-mee] -noun- An individual or a community which believes that its own nature is parallel to divine nature

Theophany [thee-of-uh-nee] -noun- When God, or a god, manifests himself to a person

Total Depravity [toh-tuhl-dee-prav-uh-tee] -noun- A doctrine which states that a fallen man is completely touched by sin and is therefore depraved

Torah [toh-ruh] -noun- In Judaism, the Pentateuch, which is the first of the three divisions of the Old Testament

Tradition [truh-dish-uhn] -noun- In a culture, the continuing of a pattern of beliefs or rituals

Tradition, Sacred [sey-krid truh-dish-uhn] -noun- A tradition in the Eastern Orthodox or Roman Catholic churches which has been handed down through generations

Traducianism [truh-doo-shuh-niz-uhm] -noun- The belief that the soul is created along with, and at the same time as, the human body

Transcendence [tran-sen-duhns] -noun- In reference to the relation of God and his creations, they are independent and different from one another

Transfiguration [trans-fig-yuh-rey-shuhn] -noun- The glorified and supernatural change shown in Jesus when he appeared on the mountain

Transcendental Idealism [tran-sen-dent-uhl-ay-dee-uh-liz-uhm] -noun- In philosophy, the teaching that a person's knowledge is achieved and learned through their senses

Transliterate [trans-lit-uh-reyt] -verb- To create a word out of the letters of a foreign alphabet

Transubstantiation [tran-suhb-stan-shee-eyt] -noun- The changing of the bread and wine given in the Eucharist to the body and blood of Christ

Tribulation, The [trib-yoo-ley-shuhn] -noun- In premillennialism, the seven years which comes directly before the return of Christ, characterized by three years of peace followed by three years of war

Trichotomy [trih-kot-uh-mee] -noun- The division of human beings into three parts: mind, body, and soul

Trinity [trin-i-tee] -noun- In Christianity, the Holy Trinity of the Father, the Son, and the Holy Spirit

Trinity, Ontological [on-tl-oj-i-kuhl-trin-i-tee] - noun- In metaphysics, the branch which explores the nature of existence

Tritheism [trahy-thee-iz-uhm] -noun- A belief in three gods; often the belief that the three sections of the Holy Trinity are three separate gods

Type, Typology [tip-ol-uh-jee] -noun- One thing's representation of another, or a study of these representations

U

Uncial [uhn-shee-uhl] -noun- The letters of the Greek alphabet which are capitalized; some Greek manuscripts of the Bible are written in uncial letters

Unitarianism [yoo-nuh-tair-ee-uh-niz-uhm] - noun- A system which advocates the unity of God, encourages the belief of what one wants to believe, and discounts the Trinity, the Holy Spirit, and the deity of Jesus

Universalism [yoo-nuh-ver-suh-liz-uhm] -noun- A doctrine which emphasizes the final salvation of all and also the fatherhood of God

Urim and Thummim [yer-uhm-and-thum-mim] -noun- Literally meaning, "light" and "perfection"; placed on the chest of a high priest as a means of communication with God

Vellum [vel-uhm] -noun- A manuscript which is writte on a calfskin, kidskin, or lambskin

Veneration [ven-uh-rey-shuhn] -noun- An honor which is given to saints in Roman Catholicism

Venial Sin [vee-nee-uhl-sin] -noun- A sin that is seen as minor, or accidental, and does not break one's covenant with God

Vestigia Trinitatas [ves-tij-ee-uh-trin-uh-tah-tahs] -noun- A theory develop by Augustine which maintains that signs of the existence of the Holy Trinity lie in all of creation

Vicar of Christ [vik-er-uhv-krahyst] -noun- The term by which a Pope is referred in Roman Catholicism

Vicarious Atonement [vahy-kair-ee-uhs-uh-tohn-muhnt] -noun- The theory of atonement which states that the sacrifice of Jesus legally satisfied the justice of God

W

Wholly Other [ho-lee uh-ther] -noun- The difference between God and everything and everyone else

Word of God [wurd-uhv-god] -noun- Used to describe both the words written in the Bible, as well as the existence of Jesus as a person

Wrath [rath] -noun- According to the Bible, the divine justice and judgment which is placed upon those who sin

Z

Zurich Agreement [zoo-rik-uh-gree-muhnt]-noun

Cover Image © Gino Santa Maria - Fotolia.com

Printed in Great Britain
by Amazon.co.uk, Ltd.,
Marston Gate.